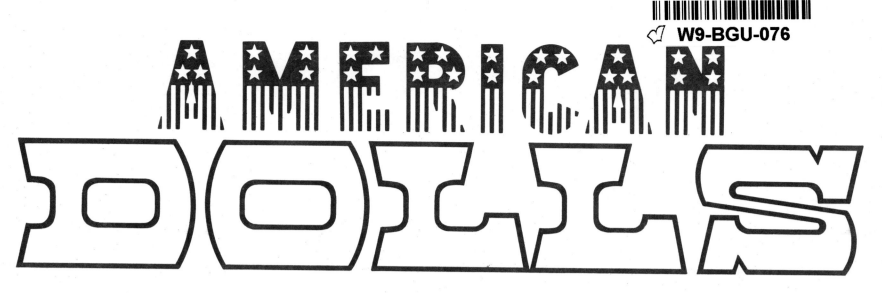

AMERICAN DOLLS

OF THE TWENTIETH CENTURY

Cisette by Madame Alexander, 1955

For Al and Zoura Martinez

WRITTEN & ILLUSTRATED BY NANCIE WEST SWANBERG

TROUBADOR PRESS
a subsidiary of
PRICE/STERN/SLOAN
Publishers, Inc., Los Angeles
1985

Schoenhut All-Wood Perfection Art Dolls

Albert Schoenhut was born to a family of German wood-carvers and toymakers. At the age of seventeen he immigrated to the United States and, in 1872, began his own toy making business producing children's musical instruments. Later he expanded the business to include the manufacture of numerous games, miniature shooting galleries, and dollhouses.

Schoenhut's first major success was with the Humpty Dumpty Circus, introduced in 1903. The Schoenhut family tells of the anonymous original inventor of the circus who appeared at Albert Schoenhut's office with three toys he'd created: a clown, a ladder and a chair. He wanted one hundred dollars in cash for the three pieces. Albert thought the circus was a great idea with a tremendous chance for commercial success. He offered the man a royalty, but the fellow refused it in preference for on-the-spot cash — he said he needed to get away from his wife! Albert paid him the one hundred dollars and launched the Schoenhut Circus which remained on the market for thirty years.

The colorful clowns and animals of the Circus were made of turned wood. The clowns' slotted hands and feet enabled them to hold onto chairs and stand on ladders. Sets included a handsome ringmaster and a porcelain-headed equestrienne. All the figures were jointed to maintain a variety of poses. The pieces of the circus came in two sizes and could be bought separately. Over a period of time a child could acquire an entire set which looked like the popular traveling circus troups of the day.

By 1911 Schoenhut's toy business had greatly prospered and he owned a large toy factory in Philadelphia. In that year he patented his first wooden play-dolls, which he called "All-Wood Perfection Art Dolls." These large and beautifully crafted dolls had joints which were specially developed by Schoenhut. Schoenhut's catalog described the device used for the joints as, "our new patent steel spring hinge, having double spring tension and swivel connection." This ingenious jointing technique allowed the dolls to attain and hold remarkably realistic poses.

The finely modeled faces of the dolls, though they appear to be hand-carved, are not. They were formed on a multiple cutting machine which followed a master mold. Schoenhut then took the machine-carved heads and put them under pressure in hot molds to smooth away any roughness. Finally, the faces were painted with washable enamel oil colors. Many of the dolls have molded and painted hair as well, some even with molded headbands, ribbons or bonnets. Others have fine mohair wigs and inserted sleep eyes. The mechanism for the movable eyes was the invention of Harry Schoenhut, one of Albert's six sons who, along with Albert's brother, all worked for the Schoenhut Company.

A well-known sculptor of the day named Graziano modeled the heads of the first All-Wood Perfection Dolls in 1911. These lovely heads depict children ranging from eight to ten years old. Younger children were also portrayed by very pretty dolls' heads created by a sculptor named Leslie between 1912 and 1916. After 1916 Albert's son Harry, having completed his art education in Philadelphia, took over the design of the company's dolls.

A famous and probably the rarest Schoenhut doll was the "Schoenhut Manikin." This figure of an older boy was designed for the use of art students, and to be used in window displays. It came either undressed or dressed as a basketball player, baseball player, football player or farm boy. The doll could be posed in a wide variety of natural poses. As with all Schoenhut dolls, the Manikin came with an ingenious stand consisting of a round metal disk with an upright peg. Each shoe and foot of the doll had one hole to receive the peg, allowing the doll to be placed in a given pose.

The Schoenhut wooden play-dolls were among the forerunners of a departure from the idealized child dolls of the 1800's. By the turn of the century, modern ideas about child psychology and the education of children led parents and dollmakers alike to look for a more lifelike kind of toy — a doll with the kind of realistic facial expressions with which a child could identify. Dolls with these more natural and lifelike faces became known as "character dolls." The Schoenhut All-Wood Perfection Dolls clearly expressed the modern attitude toward dolls in the 20th century.

A 1919 *Schoenhut display (courtesy the* Schoenhut Newsletter).

The Campbell Kids

E.I. Horsman has been called the father of the American doll industry. His story is a classic example of American business ingenuity, especially in regard to modern advertising.

Horsman had a good eye for anything with a commercial potential, and in the 1860's started a business selling games and imported dolls. Then in 1909 he bought the Aetna Doll and Toy Company, and with it the formula for a very successful doll composition. First patented by Aetna's Sol D. Hoffman in 1893, his composition was a mixture of melted glue, glycerine, zinc oxide and Japanese wax. It was extraordinarily durable, and salesmen demonstrated its unbreakability by banging the dolls' heads on the floor. Horsman marketed these dolls as "Can't Break 'Em" dolls.

The earliest and most sustained success of the Horsman Company dolls were the Campbell Kids, first manufactured in 1910. The Kids were designed by the popular illustrator Grace Drayton. Her Dolly Dingle paper dolls appeared in the *Pictorial Review* for many years. The Campbell Kids, however, are her most famous and enduring creations.

In 1904 Mrs. Drayton designed the first Campbell Kids to advertise products for the Joseph Campbell Company. After the Kids' first introduction in an ad in *Ladies' Home Journal* in September of 1905, the public was bombarded with Campbell Kid postcards, bridge tallies, placecards, lapel buttons and coloring books. Campbell Kid posters smiled from grocery store windows everywhere, and the company's mailing envelope boasted, "From the Home of the Campbell Kids." Today, Campbell Kids are still trademarks of the Campbell Soup Company.

The first official Campbell Kid doll had a composition "Can't Break 'Em" head and a stocky cork-stuffed body jointed at the shoulder and hip. The boy wore a romper and the girl a dress. The dolls were marked E.I. Horsman © 1910 on the back of the head. Dolls of this sort were sold in great numbers from 1913 to 1919. Several were sold by Sears, including the Dutch Campbell Kids and the Campbell College Kid, which was dressed in a blazer. An all-composition black Campbell Kid-type doll was manufactured about this time, and another Campbell Kid doll by Horsman, manufactured in 1925, was painted brown and dressed as an Indian.

In 1929 the American Character Doll Company purchased rights from Horsman, and a wonderful, new Campbell Kid was manufactured. This 13" all-composition doll was known as the Petite Campbell Kid. She appears on the cover of this book.

In later years the role of the Kids in Campbell's advertising varied with the times. They were used less with the advent of radio advertising in the 1930's, and were out altogether at the height of the Depression. During this period of harsh realism Carolyn Campbell, a fictional mother figure, replaced the Kids in Campbell ads. During World War II the Kids returned with patriotic slogans like "Buy War Stamps." Horsman came out with a new, 12½" fine quality, all-composition Campbell Kid in 1947. The doll is pictured on the opposite page, top right, in a somewhat modified form from 1948.

In the fifties, Campbell Kid dolls began to be made of plastics. The Ideal Toy Company was licensed to make a set of Kids in 1953 with vinyl heads and cloth bodies. Ideal and various other companies, including foreign manufacturers, produced many vinyl versions of the Kids, some as squeak toys, in the years to follow. Printed cloth dolls were also produced.

Many of the Campbell Kids made in the last three decades have been premium dolls. These dolls could be obtained for a small fee along with labels from various Campbell products. The first premium dolls were offered in 1955 to celebrate the 50th birthday of the Kids. The Colonial Campbell Kids, also premium dolls, commemorated America's Bicentennial.

From a 1914 postcard. This picture has not been previously published in a book (courtesy Campbell Soup Co.).

1910

1948

1976

Early Character Dolls

By 1910 the term "character doll" was being used to describe the new, realistic kind of doll that was to become so popular.

The earliest character dolls were made in Germany. Two women pioneered the new concept: Marion Kaulitz, whose composition and cloth dolls were first exhibited in 1909, and Kathe Krüse, who originally carved raw potatoes to use as heads for dolls she made for her own children. Eventually Krüse stopped using potatoes in favor of molded cloth. The resulting dolls are still world famous today. Another famous woman toy maker from Germany, Margarete Steiff, produced cloth character dolls during this period. And in America the German immigrant toymaker Albert Schoenhut manufactured fine character dolls of wood.

American manufacturers were especially quick and inventive in response to modern concepts in dollmaking. The sugar-sweet, idealized faces of an earlier time were discarded in favor of a fantastic variety of character faces. Their expressions ranged from laughing and smiling to pensive, pixieish or pouty. One of the first and most famous pouty faces belonged to Effanbee's Baby Grumpy. There were several versions of this doll produced over a period of thirty years. The one shown here (facing page, right) is the first of the Grumpies, introduced about 1912. He had a composition head, hands and forearms. The rest of the doll was cloth, stuffed with straw and quite primitive in structure, with large metal pins attaching arms and legs to the torso. Later versions had different bodies. Some Grumpies were all-composition. A unique all-composition black Baby Grumpy girl had three black yarn pigtails protruding from her molded composition head.

Famous doll designer Bernard Lipfert created another popular Effanbee character baby, Bubbles, in 1924. This successful baby bubbled with joy. The composition head had molded hair, sleep eyes, open smiling mouth with teeth, and adorable dimples.

In the early twenties a California sculptor named Helen Jensen designed Gladdie, shown here with Baby Grumpy. The original work of art was a cast bronze bust of her little son which she exhibited under the title "Laughing Child." A doll manufacturer who had seen the sculpture suggested to Mrs. Jensen that it would make a wonderful doll. Thus, Gladdie was produced in doll form, in both all-bisque and all-composition versions, and dressed as either a boy or a girl. The boy shown here was the more common composition version of the doll.

Frequently the original creators of character dolls were sculptors rather than doll designers, and often the character dolls were portraits of real children. Outside artists were hired by the dollmakers to come up with realistic models for doll faces. As the character doll craze caught on, the manufacturers' own doll designers came up with a tremendous and delightful variety of character-type dolls.

Even the lavish and frivolous doll clothes of the previous era were spurned in favor of the kind of clothing real children wore for school or play. Instead of elaborate Parisian costumes the new dolls wore smocks, overalls, sailor suits, rompers, raincoats and knit pullovers. Tasseled, high-heeled boots and satin slippers gave way to sturdy leather shoes and sandals.

The American dollmakers seemed to have a special knack for producing delightful, everyday wardrobes for their dolls. The Kampkins Kiddies rag dolls, made at Louise R. Kampers Studios in Atlantic City, New Jersey in the twenties, were typical in this respect. They came with wonderful wardrobes, including sunsuits and rompers, felt coats with matching cloth hats, striped socks, leather sandals with cutouts, flannel pajamas and robes and bedroom slippers. These rag dolls were not of the comical sort that we have today, but, rather, had sensitively molded and painted faces with very realistic expressions.

Dollmaking styles seem to come and go in cycles. The first character dolls were followed by a return to prettier, more idealized doll faces. Dolls in the forties often were dressed in fluffy party dresses. Dolls today tend to be dressed realistically, but unless they are portrait dolls, they rarely have realistic or natural faces. Seldom do we see a contemporary American doll that appears to be a depiction of a real child. As with the Cabbage Patch dolls, the style leans mainly towards comic character. The newest European dolls, however, are made of new, lifelike plastics, and are very realistic. So America, too, will probably be taking a turn in that direction. Doll makers, like other manufacturers, are ever-attentive to the trends in their very special art.

This 1913 *Kresge's* catalog ad features typical character dolls.

Early Stage and Screen Personalities

Toy makers have always realized the commercial potential of dolls made in the likenesses of famous people. In the last century, royalty, military heroes and famous entertainers such as singer Jenny Lind and dancer Fanny Elssler inspired doll makers. In our own century many movie and television characters have been made into dolls.

The first actor to gain worldwide acclaim through motion pictures was the great Charlie Chaplin. This beloved comedian and film maker won the hearts of the vast international silent film audience with his portrayal of a tramp character in baggy trousers and a derby hat. Even in the early days of his career, Chaplin's likeness was being reproduced in the form of a doll. Many different Charlie Chaplin dolls have been made throughout the years, and with a variety of materials. The one shown here (top right) is an early doll, made around 1914. He has painted features on a composition head and a crude cloth body, though he is charmingly dressed. It was a cheap doll in its day, but today is a valuable collectors' doll. A lot of the early 20th century American dolls were of this type, sold cheaply and in great numbers at places such as fairgrounds, and through mail-order catalogs.

In 1915 early Chaplin dolls were made by the fine toy company of Louis Amberg & Sons. One of the dolls was all cloth with a flat painted face and black wool hair. The other doll had a composition head and hands. The hair and features were molded and painted and it had a cloth body.

Included in a series of dolls representing famous Americans by Effanbee is a reissue in vinyl of a W.C. Fields doll (top left). The company first manufactured a portrait doll of the famous comedian in 1930, and it was a remarkable likeness of the actor, both in features and in dress. The original composition head was made like a ventriloquist's doll with a wire at the back of the head to lower the jaw, revealing an open mouth with teeth.

Ventriloquist's dolls were popular for many years, thanks in particular to Edgar Bergen's hugely successful character, Charlie McCarthy. Effanbee made a toy ventriloquist's doll of Charlie McCarthy in the thirties. In 1950 they manufactured a similar Howdy Doody doll in hard plastic; it too had a ventriloquist's mechanism in back to open and close the doll's mouth.

Charlie McCarthy was so popular that his image was widely reproduced, even on such items as children's clocks. His goofy sidekick, Mortimer Snerd, was a popular character whose likeness also inspired the making of dolls. Mortimer was a part of a series of new toys called Flexies invented by Ideal Toy Co. in the late 1930s. The Flexie dolls were 12½" tall, with molded and painted composi-tion heads and hands, wood torsos and feet, and flexible wire arms and legs. The two Flexies shown here (opposite page, bottom center) are Mortimer Snerd and Baby Snooks. The latter was a child character played by Fanny Brice, a famous comedienne of the twenties and thirties. During the early 1940's, when numerous uniformed dolls were produced to represent members of the various military services, Ideal produced a charming Flexie Soldier doll.

The 8" little girl (bottom, far right) is named Chunky, and was made in both black and white versions by the Sun Rubber Company of Ohio. Talented Ruth E. Newton designed a number of dolls, including this one for Sun Rubber. Her name, along with the manufacturer's, is printed on the back of the doll. This all-molded, soft vinyl, squeak-type doll was made in the early 1950's. Miss Newton also designed the delightful Amosandra doll for Sun Rubber. This little black nursing baby character was from the old *Amos 'n' Andy* radio program of the forties. The doll was made in 1949, and is marked with the name of the designer and the manufacturer and the patent number, plus the name Amosandra/Columbia Broadcasting System Inc.

The molded cat (bottom, far left) with swivel head, long-lashed sleep eyes and squeaker is a similar kind of toy, actually larger than shown here in proportion to the dolls. It was made by Arrow Rubber and Plastic Corporation, which produced many rubber and vinyl dolls from the early forties into the 1960's.

The real Charlie Chaplin dressed as The Little Tramp.

Baby Dolls and the Bye-Lo Baby

Baby dolls did not become really popular until this century. Through most of the last century little girls played with lady dolls. Then in the 1880s, pretty little girl dolls called Bébés were introduced by the great French doll-making firms. They were soon copied less expensively and in great numbers by German dollmakers. It was not until after the turn of the century that baby dolls, manufactured initially by German and American firms, attained wide popularity. They were first introduced in the character doll era before World War I, and have had a continued popularity to the present day.

A unique feature of the 20th century baby doll was the "bent-legged" position of the lower limbs. The bent legs were constructed in one piece without jointing at the knee, and were easy to string. A bent-legged baby doll could lie, sit or be placed in a very natural crawl position.

Two notable baby dolls were produced by German firms early in the century. The first of these was the wizened character doll, Baby, sometimes called the Kaiser Baby, produced by Kammer and Reinhardt in 1910. Later came the pretty, idealized, My Dream Baby, a very popular baby doll from the prolific Armand Marsailles Company. In America a "Can't Break 'Em" doll, Baby Bumps, was made by the Horsman Company in 1912. That same year Effanbee introduced its popular character doll, Baby Grumpy. In the twenties Effanbee had its first really big success with a baby named Bubbles while Horsman introduced Dimples, both designed by Bernard Lipfert.

In the thirties the Alexander Doll Company had a huge success with their Dionne Quints baby dolls. Nineteen-fifty brought the popular Baby Tiny Tears by the American Character Doll Company. The doll had a hard plastic head with molded hair and sleep eyes, and a rubber body. She was one of the first open mouth/nursing dolls, and, with tear ducts in her eyes, could also cry. In the sixties, Mattel Inc. developed baby dolls such as Cheerful Tearful, whose soft vinyl face can be changed from smiling to weeping expressions — a far cry, as it were, from the old "mamma" voice boxes in the baby dolls of my own childhood.

The most famous of all American baby dolls was the Bye-Lo Baby. She came to be called "The Million Dollar Baby" because of her stupendous success on the doll market. The doll was first modeled in wax by the sculptor Grace Storey Putnam in the likeness of an infant in a Salvation Army Home in 1919. The model was a newborn baby girl. The first toymakers approached by Miss Putnam felt that her doll was too realistic, but eventually the Borgfeldt Company of New York patented it in 1923. Bisque heads for the Bye-Lo Baby were produced by German manufacturers, and the dolls were on the market in 1925. These were quality bisque-headed dolls with inset glass eyes, celluloid hands, soft cloth bodies and pretty, long white baby dresses. Later some of the dolls were produced entirely of bisque. The final version of the head was modified to suit the doll manufacturer, and lacks some of the realism of the original wax model.

By the 1920's character dolls were no longer the rage and a more idealized doll like Armand Marsailles' My Dream Baby became the fashionable doll. Nonetheless, the Bye-Lo Baby proved to be a great success, with crowds of eager buyers lining up to purchase the doll when it first appeared in the stores. People were attracted by the fact that the doll was modeled after a real newborn baby. The manufacturer's insistence on making the doll prettier than a real newborn baby probably added to the aesthetic appeal of the "Million Dollar Baby."

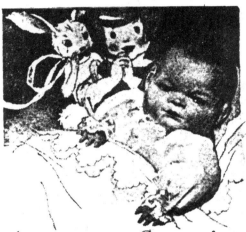

An Easter Surprise for Your Little Girl—

Can't you just imagine how delighted she will be to find a *genuine* Bye-Lo Baby Doll, like the neighbor's children have, waiting for her Easter Morning? Any imitation would disappoint her. Children never seem to tire of this wonderful doll. It's so real — so cuddlesome — so lovable — a perfect reproduction of a real three-day-old baby.

Grace Storey Putnam, the famous sculptor, studied hundreds of babies before she caught that quaint little face with its innocent loveliness.

For sale at leading toy and department stores. In seven sizes from 9 to 20 inches. Despite many poor imitations you can tell this genuine copyrighted Bye-Lo Baby Doll by the sculptor's name imprinted on the back of the head and her signature on the identification tag. If your dealer cannot supply it, write our Dept. 16A and we will tell you where you can get it.

Sole Licensee and Distributor of the Genuine "K and K" Bye-Lo Baby

Geo. Borgfeldt & Co., 111-119 East 16th St., New York

Grace Storey Putnam.

Originator of the

BYE-LO
BABY DOLL

An advertisement from a 1925 Ladies' Home Journal.

Kewpie, Scootles and Rose O'Neill

Kewpie is probably the most famous doll in the world, and its creator, Rose O'Neill, the most famous doll designer.

Rose O'Neill exhibited artistic talent early in her childhood and, even then, knew that she wanted to be an artist. She won drawing competitions for children, and by the age of fourteen was submitting poetry and art to local papers in Nebraska. Her formal art training was at the Convent of the Sisters of St. Regis in New York. She paid her own way through college doing illustrations for such periodicals as *Harper's* and *Collins Weekly*. This background prepared Miss O'Neill for a successful career as a magazine illustrator. In 1909 Miss O'Neill was asked by a *Ladies' Home Journal* editor to adapt her unique little imp-like baby drawings to a cartoon strip for children. The artist responded with a great deal of enthusiasm, calling her baby characters ''kewpies,'' a name she created as the diminutive for cupids. She said these enchanting creatures were inspired by a beloved baby brother whose ''starfish hands stretched out to reach your heart....''

She also told more romantic stories about the beginning of her Kewpies. She said, ''I dreamed them....'' She recalled that they came to her in her sleep and ''bounced about the coverlet....'' She said she knew they were elves of some sort, well-meaning and full of kindness. ''I meditated on them for days afterwards, and bit by bit, I saw they had philosophy.'' These quotes from Rose's own writings come from Rowena Ruggles' book, *The One Rose.*

The Kewpies attained immediate and widespread popularity. By October, 1912, Kewpie Kutouts were issued in book form with copies of *The Woman's Home Companion.* The first copyright for a Kewpie doll was filed for by the artist in December, 1912, and the doll was patented by March, 1913. The artist said that she tried modeling a little figurine of a Kewpie in response to requests from children who wrote and asked for a Kewpie of their very own. The original Kewpie figure had a chubby naked body with legs molded together, arms and hands outstretched, tiny wings behind each shoulder and a comical topknot. It had an impish smile with sideways glancing eyes and a snub nose.

Although Miss O'Neill selected the famous German doll manufacturer J.D. Kestner to make the first Kewpies out of fine bisque, she sculpted the first Kewpie figure herself. Eventually Kewpies were molded in a wide variety of poses, and also made as jointed play-dolls (opposite page, right).

Before World War I, there were some thirty German factories turning out bisque Kewpie dolls in great volume. The production and distribution rights for these dolls were held by George Borgfeldt and Company of New York. Eventually Kewpies were also made by the Cameo Doll Company, established in 1922. Joseph Kallus, then president of Cameo, was a well-known doll designer who worked with Rose O'Neill on the early Kewpie dolls she designed for Borgfeldt, as well as Cameo. Cameo Kewpies are being manufactured in vinyl versions of the early bisque and composition dolls. Other American manufacturers of Kewpies were Fulper Pottery, which made bisque Kewpies after World War I cut off trade with Germany, and the Mutual Doll Company which made jointed composition play-doll Kewpies.

The Kewpies became fabulously popular. Indeed, a Kewpie craze seemed to sweep the world. They sold everywhere, in authorized, as well as hundreds of unauthorized, versions. Kewpies have been made of every conceivable material, from the finest quality bisque to cloth, rubber, wood, celluloid, metal, soap, confection, composition, fairground plaster and vinyl. The Kewpie image has been reproduced on children's china, wallpaper, printed fabrics, postcards, spoon handles, lamps, inkwells and the radiator caps of cars.

Rose O'Neill created other dolls besides her Kewpies. One was a very charming baby doll called ''Scootles,'' (left, opposite) so named because, as Rose herself explained, he ''was always scooting away to adventure.'' Scootles was first produced in composition, and has now been released in vinyl.

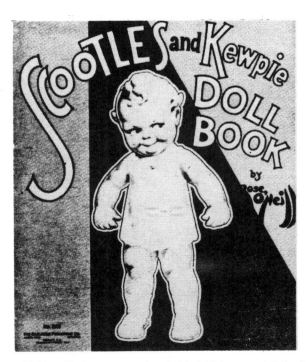

Saalfield Publishing Co. produced this 1936 paper doll book.

Skookum Indian Dolls

Skookum Indian dolls are probably recognizable to many Americans. For fifty years these dolls were manufactured in great numbers and distributed at places such as fairgrounds and rodeos. They were also used for educational purposes in schools.

Mary McAboy designed the very first Skookums using dried apples for heads. Later, heads made of papier-mâché-like composition were used. The plastic-headed Skookums of the 1950's very closely resembled the molded composition ones.

The dolls were produced in a variety of sizes, from baby Skookums, who were 4" or 5" tall, to magnificent Indian chiefs who were 3' tall! Although they are immediately recognizable as Skookums, there is an amazing variety of faces — in fact, I have never seen any two that are identical!

The Skookum Indian dolls were especially interesting for their ethnic authenticity. Though today they might be regarded by some as racial stereotypes, the attempt at authenticity was genuine, and well-crafted. The Skookums are certainly far superior to the mass-produced, cheap plastic Indian dolls that one finds in souvenir shops today.

Skookum dolls had strongly-molded faces of a dark bronze color, with hand-painted features and braided wigs of black horsehair or mohair. They wore printed cotton shirts or blouses under beautiful real woolen Indian blankets. The bodies were straw-stuffed cloth, and the arms were suggested by the folds of the blanket, padded with paper and sewn into place. The women wore printed cotton skirts and the men wore felt pants made to represent buckskin. The legs consisted of two straight pieces of rounded wood, with flat wooden feet. The earlier dolls had buckskin shoes with painted designs. The dolls from the 1950's had their feet wrapped in masking tape, or wore molded plastic moccasins. The women dolls usually carried a baby whose face peeked out from under the blanket at its mother's shoulder. The body of the baby was suggested by cloth padding under the blanket. There were also little boy and girl Skookum dolls. The costumes were based on the actual dress of the Woodland Indians of the Great Lakes region in the early 20th century.

"Skookum" is a Siwash word for "bully good." The trademark was registered by Mary McAboy for Indian Dolls in 1913, and the dolls were manufactured and distributed by Arrow Novelty Company and H.H. Tammen Mfg. Company. Affixed to the sole of a foot of each doll was a paper sticker with the declaration: Trademark Registered/Skookum/(Bully Good)/Indian/USA/Patented.

Of course, American Indians have made their own dolls. These have been handmade rather than commercially manufactured, and have been variously labeled as folk art, primitive art, and ethnic art. The Northeastern Woodland Indians made dolls of cornhusks. The Plains Indians made rawhide dolls elaborately decorated with beads. The Southwestern Indians continue to make painted, carved-wood Kachina dolls. [See *Kachina Paper Dolls* by Troubador Press.]

In dramatic contrast to the cheap souvenir dolls of today are exquisite bisque dolls that were made by the leading German doll makers before World War I. Along with some very beautiful Oriental and black dolls was a notable portrait-type doll of an American Indian girl manufactured by the firm of Armand Marseilles. Her proud, fierce, frowning figure was dressed in the fringed buckskins of the Woodlands Indians.

Such dolls are to be admired for their realism and dignity. So many "Indian" dolls have simply been white dolls painted brown and inappropriately dressed in a hodgepodge of tribal styles. Between that kind of insensitive doll making and the extreme of racial stereotyping or parody, such as the black "Mammy" doll, are ethnic dolls true to the peoples they represent. The Skookums portrayed the Indians of a certain region and time, and have been loved by several generations of children. I got my Skookum at a rodeo in Oregon when I was seven years old. He was an exotic and elegant gentleman in my playworld of dolls.

The Dionne Quintuplets by Madame Alexander

The Dionne Quintuplets were born in Canada on May 28, 1934 and became almost instantly world famous. Photographs of the five little girls, Annette, Emilie Marie, Yvonne and Cecile, were published extensively on postcards and calendars and in books and ads. The Quints' names were attached to numerous products, from foods to fans to spoons. Of course there were Dionne Quint paper dolls as well as many types of Quint play-dolls.

The loveliest of the dolls were manufactured by the Alexander Doll Company. Several sets were produced during various stages of the Quints' early childhood, from little composition infant dolls like the ones shown here, with molded and painted faces and hair, to larger toddler dolls with sleep eyes and dark wigs. The Alexander dolls were finely crafted and beautifully dressed and came with special doll furniture, such as five-seat high chairs or bassinets. Each doll's name was indicated on a pin or embroidered bib.

Madame Alexander (Beatrice Behrman) grew up in New York in the midst of the dolls of her parents' doll hospital, the first in America. Her father, Maurice Alexander, immigrated from Odessa, Russia, to Germany when he was a boy. He moved to New York in 1891, where, in 1895, he established a toy and doll repair shop. Beatrice, his eldest child, showed great artistic talent at an early age. She began designing dolls in 1915, and helped to make the Red Cross Nurse dolls sold by her father during World War I. After her marriage in 1923, Beatrice Alexander Behrman founded the Alexander Doll Company and began making dolls. Her company grew to be one of the largest and finest dollmaking companies in America.

From the beginning, Madame Alexander believed that dolls should contribute to a child's understanding of other people, places and times, as well as kindle an interest in art, literature and history.

Many of the beloved Alexander dolls were inspired by children's literary classics. Some of the charming early rag dolls depicted Alice in Wonderland, the four sisters in *Little Women* and Dickens' David Copperfield, Oliver Twist, Tiny Tim and Little Nell. Many beautiful Alexander dolls, such as Cinderella and Sleeping Beauty, were produced of fine quality composition. Since the advent of plastic dolls in the 1950's, Alexander has produced new sets of the Little Women, Alice in Wonderland and Peter Pan dolls. In 1953 Madame Alexander designed a unique set of thirty-six dolls depicting the whole coronation party of Elizabeth II. She had previously designed dolls named after the princesses Elizabeth and Margaret.

Beatrice Behrman is said to have designed all the Madame Alexander dolls throughout the years, and to have maintained strict quality control of their every detail. Her dolls are exhibited and preserved in permanent collections in museums throughout the world.

Effanbee and the Patsy Family

In 1927 the famous doll designer Bernard Lipfert introduced the original Patsy doll. Mr. Lipfert also designed the Ideal Toy Company's Shirley Temple doll.

The Effanbee Company introduced quite a number of variations on the Patsy doll between 1928 and 1940. Adding to these were the numerous "Patsy type" dolls manufactured by other companies who hopped onto the Patsy bandwagon in an eager — and successful — attempt to cash in on Patsy's enormous popularity.

The original Patsy is shown on the opposite page, second from the left. Patsy has molded hair and features, with painted rather than inset eyes, and is 14" tall. She tilts her head beguilingly to one side or the other with an impish expression. She is famous for her charming and distinctive stance, with one arm bent inward at the elbow and the other arm stretched out.

On the far left is Patsyette, the popular 9" tall member of the family. Patsyette, who first appeared in 1931, has proportionally longer and slimmer legs, with a little girl pot belly. Tall Patsy Ann at 18" (center) is a departure from the original Patsy in that she has blue, brown or green sleep eyes, rather than painted eyes. Patsy Ann was introduced as "Patsy's Big Sister" in 1928. The 11" tall doll next to Patsy Ann is Patsy Jr., introduced in 1930. Next stands Wee Patsy. This darling 6" doll was originally designed as "The Colleen Moore Fairy Princess Doll" and came in a box that was a little cardboard replica of Miss Moore's famous doll house. Wee Patsy is entirely molded and painted, even down to her white socks and black Mary Janes. Both arms are open rather than at the usual Patsy angles.

There are also a number of small bent-legged babies in the Patsy family, such as the 7" Baby Tinyette, shown on this page. A straight-legged Baby Tinyette stands at 8". Both were issued in 1933. The tallest and rarest member of the family is Patsy Mae, issued in 1935. She stands 30" tall and has sleep eyes and a human hair wig.

The dolls were produced in a tremendous variety of dress, and many of the dolls available today still have their original clothes. Most Patsy dolls wore charming children's clothes representative of the era. The Patsyette also came in a boy and girl series of historic, geographic, and storybook costumes. Wee Patsy and the baby dolls were produced in dress-alike brother and sister outfits. There were also Patsy party, riding, skating and ballet outfits, as well as other theme clothing.

One of the earliest well-loved Effanbee dolls was Baby Dainty, a charming molded and painted composition doll with cloth body. She was produced between 1912 and 1922, the later versions having tin sleep eyes. In 1924 Bernard Lipfert designed the delightful bent-legged baby doll named Bubbles. This popular doll was produced in a number of sizes and versions, and had sleep eyes, an open laughing mouth with teeth, and darling dimples. Shortly thereafter Mr. Lipfert designed another and very similar doll for Horsman Co., Baby Dimples. Effanbee sued Horsman and won its case.

Another Effanbee doll was Skippy, the comic strip character. He was introduced in 1929 as Patsy's boyfriend. In 1942 another version of Skippy was issued as a military doll and dressed in army and sailor outfits.

The American sculptor and doll designer Dewes Cochran designed a very beautiful series of dolls called the American Children Series, produced by Effanbee from 1936 to 1939. These dolls were modeled after real six and ten-year-olds and were realistically molded in very fine detail. Like the Patsys, they were made of high quality, smoothly finished composition. With their human hair wigs and in beautifully made clothes, these dolls represent the height of excellence in 20th century American dollmaking.

The Effanbee Company, founded in 1910 by Bernard E. Fleischaker and Hugo Baum, has produced some of the finest and most successful American Dolls throughout its distinguished history. In the course of eighty years it has changed owners several times, but remains one of the top American dollmakers today.

Sonja Henie and Deanna Durbin: Celebrity Dolls

Sonja Henie was born in Oslo, Norway, in 1913 and began ice skating at the age of eight. Two years later she won the first of six Norwegian figure-skating championships. She won the world's figure-skating crown for 10 consecutive years, the European title eight times in a row, and the Olympic figure-skating championship in 1928, 1932 and 1936. After that, she moved to the United States and turned professional.

Her ice skating shows attracted millions of people across the country. She wrote the autobiographical *Wings on my Feet* in 1940, and she starred in motion pictures in the thirties and forties.

The Sonja Henie doll pictured here was made of composition by the Alexander Company first in 1939, and then in three different sizes and many different costumes over a period of several years. The Alexander Sonja Henie dolls are always recognizable because of their close likeness to the star. They all have the same facial expression: a smiling face with open mouth, four teeth and dimpled cheeks. Miss Henie's dimples were to become as famous as those of the child star Shirley Temple. The dolls are marked "Madame Alexender/Sonja Henie" on the head. They are closer to a true portrait than are most Alexander dolls of the period, which tend to have a certain sameness of expression, especially because the same molds were used for a lot of different dolls. Consequently, the Sonja Henie doll is particularly valuable among collectors.

Another fine portrait doll is Deanna Durbin by the Ideal Toy Company. They made several versions in different sizes and with somewhat different molding of the faces, but the best known and most popular is the 21" version of the singing star (opposite, right). Most dolls of the early 1940's have pensive faces and little rosebud mouths, but Ideal's Deanna has a wide mouth which is open with six teeth and a felt tongue — she really looks like she's singing! The doll is beautifully made of fine quality composition. She has a luxurious dark brown human hair wig and wears a long organdy dress and a Deanna Durbin button imprinted with a photo of the star. She is marked "Deanna Durbin/Ideal Doll" on the back of the head.

The 14" Deanna Durbin mold, similar to the one described above but younger looking, was issued as the Judy Garland Teen Doll in 1941. She was marked only with "Ideal Doll" on her head. She had darker eye shadow, brown rather than green eyes, and an auburn human hair wig.

Many other stars inspired the dollmakers in this era and the years to follow. A lot of the dolls were made by the Alexander Company, which seemed particularly interested in the lavish costuming possibilities of certain screen characters. Madame Alexander always had a reputation for producing exquisitely dressed dolls, and a character like Scarlett O'Hara in *Gone With the Wind* was a natural for her. Introduced in 1939, the first Scarlett was a 14" composition doll. Though she had the usual pretty but rather expressionless face of the period, she was immediately recognizable as Scarlett O'Hara because of her green eyes, lustrous black hair and beautiful southern belle costumes. The book, by Margaret Mitchell, had been a tremendous best-seller, and its eager fans had waited two years for David Selznick to unveil the epic film version of the story. Clark Gable played the story's hero, Rhett Butler, to everyone's enthusiastic approval. Scarlett, after much speculation on the subject, was played by a beautiful newcomer from England, Vivian Leigh. The film was the most spectacular success the movie industry had ever known. Alexander came out with more Scarlett O'Hara dolls in different sizes and costumes, and of course the dolls were guaranteed to sell as long as the movie ran. In the 1950's a Scarlett was issued in vinyl, and continued to be issued in various sizes and costumes into the following decades.

From Scarlett O'Hara in the 1940's to Mary Martin as Peter Pan in the 1950's, the Beatles dolls in the 1960's and Fonzie in the 1970's (not to mention the currently popular Marilyn Monroe dolls), the stars of the world of entertainment continue to inspire dollmakers — and the public continues to delight in possessing their stars. Many of the dolls stay popular long after the stars have left the limelight.

Some of the older dolls become more and more valuable with time, like the beautiful porcelain Jenny Linds of more than a century ago. The beloved sporano toured America under the management of P.T. Barnum from 1850 to 1852. She was adored by her American public and became known as "The Swedish Nightingale." One wonders which of our present day stars will be remembered a century from now.

Front and back covers of a 1941 Sonja Henie paper doll book by Merrill Publishing Co.

Nancy Ann Storybook Dolls

Nancy Ann Abbott was born in California in 1901. The early part of her career was spent in Hollywood as a dancer, actress and dress designer. She first began sewing clothes for dolls on movie sets, making miniature replicas of the costumes worn by her actress friends, to whom she presented the dressed dolls as gifts.

In 1935 Miss Abbott opened a book lending shop on Sutter Street in San Francisco. She continued to dress little dolls in lavish costumes of her creation, and displayed and sold them in her shop. They proved to be very popular with the young working women in downtown San Francisco, and Nancy was encouraged to start a dollmaking business. At this time she met Allen L. "Les" Rowland, who gave her further encouragement and financial advice on how to establish her own business — not an easy thing for a woman to do in those days, and doubly hard during the Depression.

The Nancy Ann Dressed Dolls Company opened in 1936 and the following year Les Rowland became Miss Abbott's lifelong partner. In December, 1945, the company name was changed to Nancy Ann Storybook Dolls, Inc.

Nancy Ann Abbott started her business with a working capital of $125, working out of her own apartment at least sixteen hours a day. Soon she moved to a small shop on Howard Street. Her first dolls were tiny Hush-a-Bye Baby dolls with bodies made in Japan. Sales were good and by January, 1939, The Doll House, as the business was now known, moved to larger quarters on Ninth Street. Miss Abbott began designing and producing her famous Storybook Dolls, which illustrated nursery rhymes and fairy tales.

By 1942 the company claimed a million dollar gross yearly income and had to move once more to larger quarters that were to become its final home. Located downtown on Post Street in San Francisco, the 3-story building held a large and happy team of doll finishers and seamstresses. They belonged to the Lady's International Novelty, Handbook and Pocketbook Union, and the pay and working conditions were excellent. Employees were rotated so they wouldn't have to spend too long at one stretch doing eyestraining work on the tiny dolls and dresses.

Those were the golden years for Nancy Ann Storybook Dolls. The war didn't slow them down as much as it did so many other dollmakers. Even the U.S. government did not entirely halt their doll production — in fact, many Storybook Dolls were sent by convoy to Hawaii for the soldiers to buy as gifts for their girls back home. When doll production was cut back, the company's pottery factories made dishes for the Navy hospitals which left the company with a profitable by-product when the contract was completed.

By 1948 the Storybook Dolls appeared in plastic, but were otherwise identical to the bisque dolls, so much so that buyers and some sellers today confuse the two. A swivel head on some of the hard plastic dolls makes the only notable difference. The later plastic dolls, with their inset sleep eyes, have a very different look. They are not nearly as pretty as the painted faces.

The company branched into other kinds of dolls during the 1950's. These are attractive dolls, with a consistent high quality in their costuming, but they never gained the wide popularity of the Storybook Dolls.

In the mid-fifties, Nancy Ann Abbott became terminally ill. For eight valiant years she worked from her bed in her magnificent Hillsborough home. Her partner Les did not long survive her, and with their demise came the end of the production of Nancy Ann Storybook Dolls. But these fragile little beauties (mostly 5½" to 6½" tall) were made by the millions, and were cherished by their original owners, so that, luckily, many have survived in good condition and can be found at a reasonable price at doll shows today.

Child Movie Stars

Child stars have been a popular theme for dolls in the 20th century. Some of the early "child" stars were not children at all, but were child characters played by grown people such as the Baby Snooks character played by comedienne Fanny Brice and pictured in the form of a Flexie doll in chapter 3. Another famous child was Little Annie Rooney, played by Mary Pickford in the movie of the same name. There was a charming little bisque Annie Rooney doll made in the 1920s, with yellow yarn braids attached.

However, with the growing success of the movie industry, many popular child actors and actresses captured the imagination of doll manufacturers. Some, like Jackie Coogan, are remembered to this day. In 1921 Horsman made a Jackie Coogan doll with composition head and cloth body, dressed as he appeared in the movie The Kid.

Less of a true portrait, but better known as a doll, is the lovely Margaret O'Brien doll (opposite, left). This child star was very popular in the forties. She was especially known for her role in the 1944 Judy Garland musical, Meet Me in St. Louis. Madame Alexander first issued the doll in 1946. It was first made of composition and was reissued in the early fifties in a hard plastic version very closely resembling the original composition doll.

The Shirley Temple doll (opposite, right) was designed by Bernard Lipfert and first released at the height of the child star's fame in 1934. The perky dimpled Shirley Temple was like a living doll in the eyes of her adoring public. Many a little girl of that era had her hair curled in imitation of those famous golden ringlets. Ideal Toy Company was the lucky manufacturer of the entire line of offical Shirley Temple dolls, and produced them in great numbers throughout the 1930's. This doll remains the most fabulously successful doll ever made in America. Some 1,500,000 were sold in the 1930's alone, earning over a half million dollars in royalties for the star herself (an enormous sum in those Depression years).

The Shirley dolls manufactured from 1934 to 1940 were all-composition, with sleep eyes, an open mouth with tongue and teeth, and lavishly curled, honey-colored mohair wigs. The standing Shirley came in ten different sizes, and the bent-legged Shirley Baby came in six sizes. A rare toddler Shirley was also produced. All the Shirley Babies have side-glancing, "flirty" eyes, as do some of the standing Shirleys such as the one on the cover of this book.

Shirley Temple made thirty-one movies in her nine-year career, with Heidi, Wee Willie Winkle, The Little Colonel and Little Miss Broadway among them. New dolls were put on the market with the release of each of these new movies. The dolls were shown in photos with Shirley herself, and often dressed in look-alike outfits from Shirley's movies. There were special issue dolls such as the Shirley Sixth Birthday Doll and the Shirley Texas Centennial Ranger Doll. In 1937 the Shirley "alike" dolls appeared. These dolls were awarded to little girls who won regional Shirley Temple look-alike contests in a national competition.

One unique Shirley Temple doll was made for the promotion of the movie The Hurricane. The doll was called Marama and was chocolate brown with painted eyes, a black yarn wig, grass skirt, and lei. She represents the doll treasured by the boy Terangi because it reminds him of Marama, the role played by Shirley Temple.

Thousands of unmarked Shirley look-alikes were made by rival manufacturers trying to jump on the Shirley Temple bandwagon. These dolls tended to be of inferior quality, but, being less expensive, they too found their market. Some of the Shirley look-alikes were quality dolls, and the best of them were designed by Bernard Lipfert himself. This famous doll designer did not seem to have any reservations about developing a similar version of his own design for a rival manufacturer, a practice which resulted in several lawsuits.

By 1957 Shirley Temple films reappeared on television. Because Ideal was one of the sponsors, it obtained permission to manufacture a new Shirley doll in plastic. For the next five years the doll was produced in five sizes and dressed in various outfits, including four storybook costumes: Little Red Riding Hood, Cinderella, Little Bo Peep and Alice In Wonderland.

In 1972 there was a reissue of the 12" vinyl doll for Montgomery Ward's 100th Anniversary, and the following year a larger vinyl doll was released. The vinyl dolls do not have the value or beauty of the composition dolls of the thirties but, of course, all Shirley Temple dolls are very collectible.

Young Shirley Temple with matching doll.

Advertising Dolls

Advertising dolls appeared with the arrival of low-cost lithographic printing in the 1880's. The earliest ad dolls were mostly printed on cloth, cut out by the owner, sewn front side to back side and stuffed. These inexpensive toys still retain their popularity today.

Some of the earliest printed rag dolls were Aunt Jemima, Miss Flaked Rice and the Ceresota Flour Boy, and were offered as premiums. Some of the dolls came with the purchase of the product itself, as in the case of dolls printed on cloth flour sacks. It's fun to look at America's changing eating habits via ad dolls: from the baked goods and hot cereals that were daily fare in the early part of the century (Aunt Jemima, and Rastus the Cream of Wheat chef) to the cold cereals first developed in the 1920's, such as Kellogg's corn flakes (promoted by Goldilocks and the Three Bears dolls) and Rice Krispies (promoted by the ad dolls Snap, Crackle and Pop). One of the most famous advertising characters promoting the pre-sweetened cold cereals of modern times is Cap'n Crunch, the trademark doll promoting the Quaker Oats product of the same name.

Ad dolls have also been manufactured by toy companies and sold commercially. Some of the finest examples are the early Campbell Kids made by E.I. Horsman and American Character Doll Co. The latter company also made a charming 8" Teeny Betsy McCall doll in the mid-1950's. The Betsy shown here (opposite, top center) is made of fine quality hard plastic with rooted brown hair set in a glued-on skull cap. She has sleep eyes with molded lashes, unusual jointing at the knees and is marked ©McCall Corp. in a circle at the center of her back. She came in a wide variety of outfits.

One of the prettiest ad dolls ever manufactured was Ideal's all hard plastic Toni doll, first released in 1950 (opposite, bottom).

Designed by Bernard Lipfert, this fine quality doll promoted the Toni home permanents manufactured by the Gillette Company. She came with her own home permanent set containing a comb, a bottle of wave-set (sugar water) and tiny rollers. The lovely glued-on nylon wigs could survive a lot of styling. The dolls came in two sizes, 14" and the rarer 18", with many different outfits. The wigs came in several colors, but the most popular was the "peroxide blond" in the late 1940s and early 1950s.

Ideal sold several other dolls using the "Toni" mold. Among these were Miss Curity and Harriet Hubbard Ayers, two other ad dolls. Miss Curity promoted Curity first aid products. Harriet Hubbard Ayers was the ad doll for a line of cosmetics of the same name.

A doll whose manufacturer remains unknown is Buddy Lee, the ad doll for Lee jeans (opposite, top left). The H.D. Lee Company will not reveal the name of their doll's manufacturer, nor has any company claimed to be the maker of Buddy Lee — a situation forever frustrating to doll collectors and historians! Buddy Lee is a fine quality doll both in composition and in the later hard plastic version.

The dolls were first sold in 1922 to dealers as display dolls, to promote Lee work clothes and industrial uniforms. Seventeen different outfits were manufactured by the Lee company for their doll. Caps, belts and other accessories were made by outside sources.

Buddy was most popular in his cowboy outfit shown here. Besides the cowboy, the best-known Buddys are the Engineer, the Farmer and the Coca-Cola Buddy. Lee custom-manufactured industrial uniforms for a number of large companies. Along with the popular Coca-Cola uniform, there were uniforms in miniature for Phillips 66, Standard Oil and John Deere.

Such a high quality doll and clothes eventually became too expensive to manufacture and sell at a reasonable cost, and by 1962 the Buddy Lee Doll was discontinued. Present-day collectors have begged for a reissue of the doll, but the company has recently stated that it has no plans to reissue Buddy Lee.

The Gerber Baby (opposite, top right) was based on an original 1928 drawing by Dorothy Hope Smith. After its introduction in 1936, a long succession of Gerber Baby dolls followed in various sizes and materials. Several were manufactured by the Sun Rubber Company, including an 18" doll offered in the Sears Catalog in 1955. Most Gerber Babies came with a baby bottle and were nursing and wetting dolls like the one pictured here. This 11" vinyl doll, made by Uneeda in 1972, came with a plastic high chair, dish and bottle. The white baby had yellow hair rather than the brown hair of all previous Gerber Babies. A black Gerber Baby was made from the same mold. Many toy companies have produced black and white dolls using the same mold. Another ad doll to be made in both black and white versions was the Campbell Kid.

Buddy Lee dolls dressed in cowboy, shirt-pants and union-all outfits.

Dolls from the Comics

Comic books and syndicate comic strips are a 20th century American invention. The daily exposure to hundreds of millions of fans makes comic characters a sure subject for doll manufacturers.

The list of comic strip dolls is a long one. Uncle Walt and Skeezix from "Gasoline Alley," Skippy, Henry, Blondie and Dagwood, Mutt and Jeff, Popeye, Li'l Abner, the characters from "Peanuts," Mickey Mouse and Garfield, just to name a *few*.

"Bringing Up Father," drawn by George McManus, began in 1913. The first version of Jiggs and Maggie from this early strip were made of painted and jointed tin, with fabric clothes. Another set of dolls by Schoenhut was made of jointed, painted wood. Popeye and Olive Oyl were also made in both tin and wood. There is a jointed, soft vinyl Popeye made by Cameo in the late fifties, not to mention the figures in pottery and molded plastic that have been manufctured since the feature film "Popeye" renewed this character's popularity in the late 1970's.

Little painted bisque characters from Frank King's strip, "Gasoline Alley," were made in the early 1920's. In 1927 the Sears Catalog offered dolls of Skeezix and his dog, Pal. They were made of printed oilcloth. The stuffed cloth dolls of Nancy and Sluggo are from the strip by Ernie Bushmiller (opposite, left and right) are similar to the much earlier Skeezix doll in that they too are quite flat, with printed front and back sides and were made by Knickerbocker in 1973.

Little Lulu (third from the left), the comic book character created by Marjorie Buell, is shown in a printed cloth version. I have seen a number of different Little Lulu dolls, all unmarked, but they have all been rag dolls with black yarn hair and either painted or embroidered faces. Little Orphan Annie and her dog Sandy have also been made in several cloth versions, including an oilcloth version like the Skeezix doll. Orphan Annie has been produced as a doll, figurine and wind-up toy. She's been made of bisque, tin, composition and celluloid, as well as cloth and wood.

The last two dolls in the picture were made by that prolific manufacturer of popular dolls, the Ideal Toy Company. Both are characters from the "Dick Tracy" comic strip by Chester Gould of *The Chicago Tribune*. Sparkle Plenty was "born" in 1947. Her parents were two infamous characters in the strip, tobacco-chewing B-O Plenty and his bug-eyed wife Gravel Gertie. This shining child with the long golden hair was an instant hit in the comics and Ideal, always quick to spot a winner, had its 15" Sparkle Plenty doll on the market that same year.

Sparkle's head was of hard plastic and was marked with Ideal's patent number for that material, which was brand new at the time. The body was made of another new material, a very soft latex called "magic skin" by the doll manufacturers. A number of companies, including Alexander, used this material for doll bodies in the late forties. The surface of these soft, stuffed latex bodies felt magically like real skin. Little did the manufacturers or their unsuspecting customers know that "magic skin," when exposed to the sun, turned dark brown! So there was Sparkle, with her pale face, blue eyes and long yellow yarn hair, after a summer of being played with outdoors, turned spotty brown from the neck down. The use of "magic skin" was quickly abandoned by the manufacturers. Most Sparkle Plentys found today have had their heads put on vinyl bodies which are not original.

Bonnie Braids (fourth from the left), the child of Dick Tracy and his wife Tess, was "born" in 1951. The doll was made in several versions through 1953. The first had painted features and a "magic skin" body. Later models had sleep eyes and vinyl bodies, like the doll shown here. All Bonnie Braids dolls are recognizable by their unique facial expressions and hair styles. An open, laughing mouth reveals three painted teeth. Two little yellow beribboned braids are made of one piece of saran hair pulled through a hole high on each side of the head. The head is marked "Chicago Tribune/Ideal Doll," and the year of manufacture.

Like so many American dolls, the comic dolls give three-dimensional life to their fictional, cartooned, counterparts and bring their special magic into the play of millions of enchanted children.

Barbie

The Barbie* made by Mattel Inc. tells the ultimate success story of a contemporary doll. A little known fact is that the prototype for Barbie* was a European doll named Lilli. A German firm, inspired by a newspaper cartoon character, created the Lilli doll, then sold it to Mattel. In 1959 Mattel introduced their version as Barbie.*

Barbie* was soon joined by her boyfriend, Ken,* little sister, Skipper,* and brother, Ricky,* and various friends, including the black doll, Francine.* These shapely, long-legged, dolls have large and very contemporary wardrobes, furniture, cars — even swimming pools and fold-out apartments! Along with these larger items are numerous small accessories such as telephones, transistor radios, television sets, dishes, magazines, surfboards, suitcases — a seemingly endless array of accoutrements. The manufacturer is continuously adding to the available wardrobes and accessories, so that once a little girl owns a Barbie* there is no end to the things she may acquire for her doll. Consequently, the commercial success of this doll and others of her kind is assured and enormous.

The Barbie*-type doll is a departure from the little girl and baby dolls of the previous several decades. She represents a return to the lady doll, or a doll with a more adult figure. She also expresses a contemporary trend to cultivate the teenage market. Barbie* is the ultimate sophisticated contemporary teenager, and the little girls who play with her can identify with her as the perfect young woman they wish one day to become.

By now many countries have their own versions of Barbie.* In France, there is the seductive Silvie. In England, there's sporty Sindy and her kid sister Patch. In a way, these very contemporary dolls are like the French fashion doll of over a hundred years ago with her Saratoga trunk full of fashionable clothes and accessories. Of course, silk and velvet and woolen fabrics have been replaced with modern synthetics, and our great-grandmothers would be scandalized by the skimpy bikinis and pink plastic sunglasses worn by Barbie* and her friends.

Ken* and the other Barbie* boyfriends serve mainly as accessories to the girl dolls, and are played with by little girls. But there are many Barbie*-type contemporary dolls made especially for little boys. G.I. Joe® **, made by Hasbro, was first manufactured in the 1960's, during the time of the Vietnam War. He is a modern example of a doll which has always existed for boys — the toy soldier. Called "America's movable fighting man," G.I. Joe® ** came outfitted as a soldier, marine, sailor, or pilot. Accurately uniformed, and equipped with a cartridge belt, M1 rifle and hand grenades, he was very popular with little boys whose fathers and brothers were fighting a real war. It is interesting to note that since the end of the Vietnam War, American boys seem more interested in the molded vinyl dolls made in the likenesses of popular adventure/fantasy film characters, such as the characters from the *Star Wars* series. We can hope that the natural aggressions inherent in all children can continue to be played out with the inspiration of fictional, rather than actual, wars.

In any case, contemporary dolls will always be an expression of our values and ideals as well as of current fashions, events and personalities, whether fictional or real. As such they constitute a fascinating and charming glimpse of their time in history.

*Trademarks and copyrights of Mattel, Inc. used with permission.
**©1985 Hasbro Bradley, Inc.

Bibliography

Anderton, Johana Gast. *Twentieth Century Dolls*. Wallace Homestend, 1971.

Axe, John. *The Encyclopedia of Celebrity Dolls*. Hobby House Press.

Coleman, D.S., E.A., and E.J. *The Collector's Encyclopedia of Dolls*. New York: Crown Publishers, 1968.

Coleman, D.S., E.A., and E.J. *The Collector's Encyclopedia of Doll Clothes*. New York: Crown Publishers, 1975.

Desmonde, Kay. *All Color Book of Dolls*. Octopus Books, Ltd. London, 1974.

Eaton, Faith. *Dolls in Color*. Macmillan Publishing Co., Inc., New York, 1975.

Foulke, Jan. *EFFanBee Composition Dolls*. Hobby House Press, 1978.

Fox, Carl. *The Doll*. New York: Henry Abrams, 1972.

Fraser, Antonia. *A History of Toys*. Delacorte Press, 1968.

Hillier, Mary. *Dolls and Dollmakers*. New York: Putnam's Sons, 1968.

King, Constance Eileen. *Dolls and Doll Houses*. London/New York: Hamlyn, 1977.

King, Constance Eileen. *Collectors History of Dolls*. New York: Bonanza /Crown Publishers, 1977.

Noble, John. *A Treasury of Beautiful Dolls*. New York: Hawthorn Books Inc., 1971.

Manos, Paris and Susan. *The World of Barbie Dolls*. Collector Books, 1983.

Miller, Marjorie A. *Nancy Ann Storybook Dolls*. Hobby House Press, 1980.

Robison, Joleen and Sellers, Kay. *Advertising Dolls*. Collector Books, 1980.

Ruggles, Rowena Godding. *The One Rose*. 1964.

Smith, Patricia R. *Modern Collector's Dolls*. New York: Crown Publishers, Inc., 1973.

St. George, Eleanor. *The Dolls of Yesterday*. Charles Scribner's Sons, Ltd., New York, 1948.

Special thanks to: Mr. and Mrs. M. P. Maynard, Suzanne Lyons and Marlo Brown for access to their private doll collections; Marian P. Garrison and Frank A. Dudowicz of the Campbell Soup Co.; Lee Jeans; Mary Young; American Doll Co.; *The Schoenhut Newsletter*; and the *Chicago Tribune*.

© Mattel Inc. 1958, 1960

© Mattel Inc. 1968, 1979

© Mattel inc. 1966

More Imaginative Books from Troubador Press

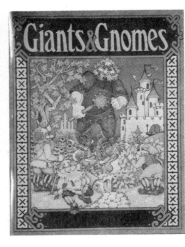

YOUNG READERS

A Child's American Heritage	$2.95
Draw Your Own Monsters	2.95
Fairy Tales	2.95
It's Your World	2.95
Meanings of Christmas	2.95
Nature Crafts & Projects	2.95
Party & Picnic Cookbook	2.25
Troubador Treasury	4.95
Windows of Nature	2.95

CREATIVE CUT-OUTS

Alien Starships	$3.50
Everything For Your Birthday Party Book	3.95
Flashback Fashion Paper Dolls	3.95
Geometric Playthings	3.95
Gorey Cats Paper Dolls	3.95
Great Ballet Paper Dolls	3.95
Kachinas Paper Dolls	3.95
Magic Tricks	3.95
Paper Airplanes	3.95
Paper Movie Machines	3.95
Paper Robots	3.50
Paper Rockets	3.95
Paper Starships	3.95
Paper UFOs	3.95
Pinwheels	2.50
Teddy Bear Paper Dolls	3.95
3-D Optical Illusions	3.95

GAMEBOOKS

Big Book of Board Games	$3.50
Dinosaur Fun Book	2.95
Famous Monster Fun Book	2.95
Gnomes Fun Book	2.95
Gnomes Games	4.50
Gorey Games	4.50
In Visibles	2.95
In Visibles 2	2.95
Maze Craze	2.95
Maze Craze 2	2.95
Maze Craze 3	2.95
Maze Craze 4	2.95
Mother Goose	2.95
Puzzlers	2.95
3-D Maze Art	4.95
3-D Mazes	2.95
3-D Mazes, Vol. 2	2.95
3-D Monster Mazes	2.95

COLOR & STORY

Aesop's Fables	$3.95
Ballet	3.95
Bears	3.95
Beasties	3.95
Butterflies & Moths	3.95
Cats & Kittens	3.95
Cowboys	3.95
Dinosaur	3.95
Dogs & Puppies	3.95
Dolls Through the Ages	3.95
Double-Ups	3.50
Enchanted Forest	3.95
Enchanted Kingdom	3.95
Giants & Gnomes	3.95
Good Times America	3.95
Horse Lovers	3.95
Hot Air Ballooning	3.95
Los Angeles Coloring Album	3.95
Love Bug	3.50
Monster Gallery	3.95

Mother Goose	3.95
North American Birdlife	3.95
North American Indians	3.95
North American Sealife	3.95
North American Wildflowers	3.95
North American Wildlife	3.95
Puggle Tales	3.95
Reptiles & Amphibians	3.95
San Francisco Scenes	3.95
Space WARP	3.50
Tales of Fantasy	3.50
World of Horses	3.95
Zodiac	3.50

GIFT

How To Draw Prehistoric Monsters	$3.95
How to Draw Robots & Spaceships	4.50
Optricks	2.95
Scrimshander	9.95
Stereo Views	7.95
Travels with Farley	6.95

For a complete list of titles, send us your name and address.

Troubador Press books are available from book, gift, toy, art material, museum and department stores, or may be ordered directly from the publisher.

Send your check or money order for the total amount plus $1.00 for handling and mailing to:

TROUBADOR PRESS
a subsidiary of
PRICE/STERN/SLOAN
Publishers, Inc., Los Angeles